de KANSAS a CALIFAS & back to CHICAGO

Carlos Cortez Koyokuikatl

MARCH/Abrazo Press
Chicago

Acknowledgements

"Quo Vadisimus?" and "Yosemite" first appeared in *Emergency Tacos: Seven Poets Con Picante* (MARCH/ Abrazo Press, Chicago, 1989); "Poema Por El Dia De La Raza" appeared in *ART PAPERS*, Volume 16, Number 1, Jan./Feb., 1992; "Mojave, Califas," "Puridad," "Laguna," "Two December Songs for 1982," and "Soledad, Califas," were published in *Notebook: A Little Magazine*, Raza Cosmica issue, Volume 4, Number 2; "Tehachapi Pass," *Industrial Worker*, July, 1988.

Copyright © 1992 by Carlos Cortez
Second printing, 1994

All rights reserved. No part of this book may be reproduced in any manner without written permission of the author, except for quotations contained in articles or reviews.

Scratchboard art: Carlos Cortez Koyokuikatl
Book design: Cynthia Gallaher

Library of Congress Cataloging-in-Publication Data

Cortez, Carlos, 1923—

    De Kansas a Califas & back to Chicago
    I. Title   II. Poetry   III. Chicano art

92-060876   1992

ISBN 1-877636-09-6 (pbk.)

The paper used in this book meets the requirements of the American National Standard for Permanence of Paper for Printed Library Materials.

Para Marianna

Table of Contents

Foreword / 5
Elk City Night Stop / 9
Laguna / 10
Quo Vadisimas? / 12
Puridad / 15
Tehachapi Pass / 16
Yosemite, 1982 / 18
Yosemite Night Scene / 19
Night on Highway #1 / 22
Untitled / 23
Soledad, Califas / 25
Mojave, Califas / 26
Pomona / 28
Untitled / 30
Club El Mercado / 32
Centinela / 35
Tumbleweeds / 38
Tumbleweeds #2 / 40
Two December Songs for 1982 / 44
Poema for El Dia de la Raza / 45

Foreword

Carlos Cortez Koyokuikatl is what is sometimes called a "timeless one."

In essence, the song he sings has been with us forever. I am convinced that his song will remain with us for as long as there is an ear to hear it.

Even after all ears are gone, the song Carlos sings will still ride the stars.

It is the coyote's song (Koyokuikatl).

Now, that song sometimes jars the so-called sophisticated ear. What does that say about sophisticated ears? Perhaps it says that sophisticated ears have lost the ability to appreciate that which is simple—the desert, the cloud, the cactus flower, hot chile, the bright blue sky, the tumbleweed, the hammering sun, and the song of the coyote.

The poems of Carlos Cortez are simple. Not only the poems in this volume. All of his poems. I believe I've read and heard most of them. I've been reading and hearing them for thirty years—which is to say, ever since I first met him.

There is nothing obscure about his poems. No one has to scratch head and puzzle around trying to figure out what Carlos means, what he's trying to communicate. Nor is there ever any doubt that his poems are intended for all people. He has no special audience. He's not trying to impress anybody. His poems are for you—and for me—and for the hitchhiker down the counter there nursing a cup of coffee.

Carlos feels a connection to everything that lives. The mountain cat becomes a fellow living being to all of us in these lines: "May your Grandchildren/Teach your assassins/The proper path." In my opinion, that is true poetry.

These poems deserve to be read—and read again—and read again.

I identify deeply with the poems in this collection. They were written on a trip to California and back to Kansas which Carlos took with me and my wife and our deaf white dog in the closing months of 1982. We made the trip in a used camper. We stopped here, we stopped there. We met Wobbly brothers in Albuquerque. We ate bad food in a fast-food joint on the edge of the Mojave Desert. We saw smog in Pomona. We watched the sun set over the Pacific near Half Moon Bay. (I will never forget the sight of Carlos facing west, perfectly still, in humble acceptance, listening to the breathing of the Great Spirit.) We spent time with my daughters in San Francisco and with union friends in Oakland. We enjoyed getting to know the people in Santa Cruz. We ate proper food in Soledad. We slept next to the saguaro in Stanfield, Arizona. And we were, as always, *compadres* —just as we have been ever since we first met thirty years ago.

I am delighted to see these poems in print. I'm pleased to be able to hear their song once more.

I am very proud that Carlos asked me to write this Foreword.

Thank you, Carlos.

And I know that after you have read these poems, have looked at the accompanying art, you will thank him, also.

Joel Climenhaga
Dieciseis de Septiembre, 1991

Elk City Night Stop

The barreling semi-trucks,
The autos,
The sprawling suburbia of motels
With air-conditioned closed-circuit TV;

I hear the thunder of hoofbeats:
The Buffalo are coming back!

Laguna

After exasperating miles
Of tourist-trap freeway-avenues
The sight of a cluster of adobe houses
On a hillside
Blending with the terra cotta
Landscape,
A harmony that is not even disturbed
By the contrast of a whitewashed
Spanish mission
Is a melodious but firm reminder
That people were born
To blend with the Earth.

Quo Vadisimus?

The West ain't what it used to be
And it's getting ain'tier every day;
All those small bus stop towns
That had a special place en mi corazón,
(Never mind the long history of hassle
Contra Raza y Indigena)
Have become obscene imitations
Of Las Nalgas and Miami Bitch;
Swimming pool and closed-circuit TV motels,
Colonel Sandhog and MacDunghills,
With authentically expensive
Indian curio shops,
(Mientras los Indios fueron desempleados
So damn long they can't afford to
Emborrachar anymore) y los
Fancy cafés and clubs strung along the freeways
All after the bucks of the bored suburbanites
And I can't find a sack of Bull Durham
Anywhere!

quo vadisimus—where are we going?
corazón—heart; core
contra raza y indigena—against the race (Mexicans) and the indigenous
Las Nalgas—(Las Vegas) the buttocks
mientras los Indios fueron desempleados—meanwhile, the Indians have been unemployed
emborrachar—get drunk

Puridád

And then comes the Desert,
The pure clean Desert,
That great fullness
That reminds the frantic motorists
Of their own EMPTINESS

Mojave Desert, 1982

Tehachapi Pass

You used to be able to see
The Mountains on the other side
Of the Valley...
But now you long
For the clean Desert air
As you watch the smog
Drifting up from Los Angeles.

I hear the flapping of wings;
The California Condor is coming back,
Even if he has to migrate
From Machu Picchu!

Yosemite, 1982

The bark houses,
The stone mortars,
A complete village
Just like the old days;
All for the tourists!

But the entrances to the
Ceremonial house
And the Sweat Lodge
Are closed off!
They are still in use!

Wa chi taw!
It is good!

Yosemite Night Scene

In the high Sierras
Night comes quickly;
The tall Pines
And the
Taller Mountains
Sing to me:

Solitude can be
The greatest company!

Night on Highway #1

The dark sky
And the dark Ocean
Shine brightly
Around
The even darker
Mountain;

¡Que poderosas
Son las montañas!

Another rainy day
   in San Francisco;
My warmth
   is far away!

Soledad, Califas

Soledad quiere decir,
Solitude en Inglés
Pero no hay ningún loneliness
En este pueblito
Off the main highway
En Califas.

En "El Zacatecano"
Onde comí mis huebos con chorizo
While looking at
And listening to the mariachis
On the TV from Salinas
And looking at the Ventana Mountains
Through the front window,
Hay mas pica que el chile.

Out on the distant highway
The Twentieth Century speeds on
To its ultimate oblivion
Pero aqui hay Raza
Por todos lados.

Never mind the history books,
Dice la Palomita,
We never lost Califas!

Mojave, Califas

In the roadside café
A stuffed Mountain Lion stands
With a hand-lettered card,
"Thank you for not touching!"
Pero, Hermanito,
You have already been touched!

How long must such
Indignity continue?

Spirit of the Mountain Cat:
May your Grandchildren
Teach your assassins
The proper path!

Pomona

Like a morning ghost
The snow-capped
Gabrieles
Loom above
The palm trees and
Cottages and motels
And smog
Of the car-culture
Streets
Ever reminding
That eternity
Is NOW!

17 Noviembre, 1982

Never mind;
High above
The smog
The Mountains
Are still
THERE!

17 Noviembre, 1982

Club El Mercado

Cuando moriré
No me importa
Si San Pedro
Me dice
"Vete pa'l otro piso, ese"
Si hay Mariachis allá.
Y si no hay...
Si todos seran a la Gloria;

No seré el primer indocumentado
Que pasar pá
Las Pearly Gates.

20 Noviembre, 1982

Centinela

Beneath the high street lamp
In the overnight
Trailer park;
With the encouragement
From the Desert Moon;
The young Saguaro
Maintains his unapproachable
Dignity.

28 Noviembre, 1982
Mile 151, Arizona

Tumbleweeds

When the Tumbleweed
Has finished his days of existence,
The roots that bind him down
To the Earth Mother
Give way
And he can go wherever
The Winds take him.

How much better
Than a tombstone
And the Pearly Gates!

Tumbleweeds #2

Tumbleweeds
Dancing along the Texas highway.
Only flatlands and wheatfields ahead!

Ontá mis adoradas Montañas?
No more Saguaro, también.

¡Solo tus brazos
Me pudieron consolar!

Two December Songs for 1982

I.
Snaking around the block
From the Unemployment Compensation
Office
The early morning waiting line
Of new applicants
Look at the Christmas decorations
On the businesses across the street
While telling the canvasser from
Voter registration to go to Hell
As Booger King's Stars and Stripes
Are whipped into further ragged tatters
By the cold December wind.

II.
Praise SOMEBODY for
Little blessings!

Here
They do a better job
Of calling out surnames
Than down at
Immigration Service!

Poema por El Dia de la Raza

Mucho siglos antes los Chinos
    came to these shores
And saw that they were not
    the first people that came here.
For many Moons they sailed along
    the Pacific Coast
Taking notes for their history books,
    swapping semillas, cuentos y palabras
Before sailing back to China.

Some centuries later some Scandanavians
    came across the other Ocean,
Real rough batos who were accustomed
    to coming on pretty tough
But when they found out that those whom
    they called the Skraelings
Could be every bit as rough, they sailed back
To their fjords and flaxen-haired rucas.

It has been rumored that some Celtics
    also sailed over
    and must have liked what they saw
Because it has further been rumored that they
    stayed around and became
Light-skinned Indians because it is rumored
That they never bothered to go back to Wales.

All of the early navigators knew, be they
    güero Vikings, prieto Polynesians
    o quien sabe quien,

That when Mountains disappear
    beneath one horizon
    or rise up from another horizon,
This Earth of ours cannot be flat;
So never mind what the school teachers
    try to tell you,
Este cabrón,
    Cristobal Colón,
        Cristóforo Colombo,
            Christopher Columbus,
Whatever your particular ethnocentric bias
    chooses to call him,
He did not think of anything new.

Si el Rey y la Reina de España really believed
This Earth of ours was as flat as a tortilla,
They wouldn't have given old Chris
    any second thoughts,
Pero con sus corazones de ladrones
    they recognized in this fregón
Immense possibilities of empire
    or they would have never
Invested any of their parasitic wealth
    in his grandiose idea.

Pero aquél Cristobal, his reputation as a
    sea captain was so notorious that
The only way he would have any crew at all
Was for their majesties to man his three ships
    with "volunteers" from the
Spanish prisons and the invasion
    was soon under way.

Since that day that old Chris landed on these shores
    and thought he was meeting the sons of Krishna,
Some sinvergüenza with a badly-misplaced
    sense of humor
Has designated for posterity
    as "El Dia de la Raza,"
Pero guachale, even Raza cannot remember
    when Raza first came to these shores
And even if some of us have become mezclados con
    Español, Portugués, Africano, Francés o Anglo-Sajón,
    one thing we know fo' shu'
La Raza did not begin in 1492!

Their historians refer to us as primitive, backward
    and historically unprogressive,
Pero nuestro maiz, papas, gitomates, calabazas, tabaco,
    chocolate, camotes, vanilla, chiles y cacahuates,
Saved their so-called "Old World" from certain
    starvation and probable revolution;
Helped them to feed their hungry armies and navies
    so they could be progressive enough
    to colonize the World.

Yes, it can be said that we backward and
    historically unprogressive descamisados
Have done our part towards bringing into being
    capitalism and the "modern age,"
Though we would much prefer to be
    remembered for jamacas, toboggons y elotes.

Pero para nosotros, "El Dia de la Raza"
    todavia no lo llegue;
It is still somewhere in the future.
In spite of cannon balls, gatling guns, bullets,
    missionaries, rot-gut whisky,
        typhoid and small pox-infested blankets,
        scalpel-happy abortionists and the
        bad arithmetic of the census takers,
We are still around and we intend to stick around
    for quite a while longer
    and for a damn good reason;
You see, we were practicing ecology and
    the classless society for
    thousands of years before
Our "civilizers" even had words for these things!

¡Itzachilatlan aik ixpolihuiz!

mucho siglos antes los Chinos—   many centuries before; the Chinese
semillas, cuentos y palabras   —seeds, stories and words
rucas —girls (gals)
qüero —blond
prieto —dark; swarthy
o quien sabe quien   —or who knows who
sinvergüenza —shameless
ladrones —theives

photo by Alejandro Galindo

Carlos Cortez

Carlos Cortez' first book, *Crystal Gazing the Amber Fluid: & Other Wobbly Poems,* was awarded the Kwanzaa Award.

MARCH/Abrazo books are available to the trade from Baker & Taylor Co. and library jobbers.

Books can also be ordered directly from the publisher. For orders, a catalog, or more information on live performances, write to:
MARCH/Abrazo Press
P.O. Box 2890
Chicago, Illinois 60690-2890